Veronica Aaronson

Veronica
Xmas 2020

Nothing About The Birds
Is Ordinary This Morning

Indigo Dreams Publishing

First Edition: Nothing About The Birds Is Ordinary This Morning
First published in Great Britain in 2018 by:
Indigo Dreams Publishing
24, Forest Houses
Halwill
Beaworthy
Devon
EX21 5UU

www.indigodreams.co.uk

Veronica Aaronson has asserted her right under the Copyright, Designs and Patents Act 1988 to be identified as the author of this work.
©2018 Veronica Aaronson

ISBN 978-1-910834-96-1

British Library Cataloguing in Publication Data. A CIP record for this book can be obtained from the British Library.

Designed and typeset in Palatino Linotype by Indigo Dreams.
Cover artwork by Gay Anderson.

Printed and bound in Great Britain by 4edge Ltd.
www.4edge.co.uk

Papers used by Indigo Dreams are recyclable products made from wood grown in sustainable forests following the guidance of the Forest Stewardship Council.

For my grandchildren: Lily, Eloise, Bear, Sam
and any that might follow.

Acknowledgements

My deep thanks goes to Jennie Osborne who helped me into my poetry skin. A special thanks to Matthew Aaronson and Kim Bour for keeping me buoyant whenever I lost faith in my ability and for their inspiration and guidance. Also to my editing group – Edward Aldous, Sheila Aldous, Virginia Griem and Jean Grimsey and to Robin Aaronson who has the patience of a saint and is my constant support. Finally to everyone who attends Poetry Teignmouth evenings – these evenings have extended my knowledge and love of poetry.

Nothing About The Birds is Ordinary This Morning
is Veronica Aaronson's first collection.

CONTENTS

Nothing About The Birds Is Ordinary This Morning

*Let us dream of evanescence, and linger
in the beautiful foolishness of things.*

– Doris Egan

On Leaving Home

It stings me before I see it,
a honey bee caught in my fringe,
eyelid burns, swells, shuts.
Other eye is blurred by cataract.
It's difficult to focus.

Is this a message not to take sight for granted,
an invitation to turn my gaze inward,
a hint of a transformation to come,
a millstone to turn my journey into a pilgrimage,
or simply the needless death of a bee?

Misfit

In the taxi line I'm out of step with the Friday night fever
of open-shirted men, barely-clothed women
drunk on the idea of the night to come. They're as tight,
as intense as tango dancers. I'm spent –
nag of injured eyelid, jostle and jolt of carriage,
wheels droning against track.

As a man with cupped hand cajoles everyone in turn,
we all set our eyes elsewhere, rehearse what to say,
decide whether to give. He ignores the youth
can in hand, slumped on the pavement
with a White Lightening glow

and asks nothing of me, instead gives a nod of recognition,
as if my listless body, eyelid weighted down
with bee sting ballast, tells my whole story.

Having Arrived Despite Choppy Seas

A cormorant skims water.
A ginger cat rubs his back
against sun-heated stones.

I crunch through meringue,
listen to the lulling
of a fishing rod swisshh
as a lone teenager
flicks it backwards,
a humm as he lets out the line,
each refrain marked
by the plopp of his lure.

Small cumulus clouds
sit perfectly still
one above the other,
like smoke signals
that have been stopped
in their tracks.

It's as if
some unknown danger
has been averted.

Despite Difference

On top of sand dunes
I feel unsafe, like washing
pegged carelessly in gusting wind,
like the days after my father was gone.

Even though I tramp and he marched,
I pick up pebbles, he collected silver,
I recite Rumi, he babbled Bible,
I dress in purple and he donned khaki,
now his journey's over
I really miss the rocky terrain
of our shared nothing-in-commonness.

At the base of sand dunes
I search for stones
speckled with silver.

On the North Beach

wide-awake blue draws a distinct horizon,
no wishy-washy melting of pale aqua into grey.
Waves weave a lace petticoat with each thrust forward,
unpick it as they recede, as if they can't decide
whether bare sand is indecent in this holy place.

I've gazed at waves often but in this space
I sense Moon's pull, Earth's spin.
I'm swaddled in sound –
my in and out breath in time
with tide's swish, wash, swish, wash.

I close my eyes,
take in the offering
through skin.

If Only ...

On the coastal path where fierce gusts expose
white underbellies of bramble leaves, shake
heather and gorse, flap scarves, puff out jackets,
my eyes home in on the small frame of a kestrel
taking on the wind.

This falcon hangs over the exact same spot
as if it's fixed in place by invisible wires.
Its concentration so alive its wings and tail feathers
find their own way to twist and turn in tune
with the turbulent air.

If I could hold my ground, face the gale
of his bluster, maybe my lips could find their way
to tell him how it is for me. The image runs,
re-runs. I no longer feel the cold, hear the sea
hurling abuse at the cliffs.

Playing with a Möbius Strip

Like a hummingbird hawk-moth starved of nectar
I'm pulled towards the crimson cones of a buddleia
showing off against the stone wall's muted colours of
sparrow's breast, rook's wing, bullfinch chest.

A spent tulip stalk is bullied less by wind's
push and shove than the rosa rugosa stems.
At home rosa rugosa fingers have slipped through
the wrought iron seat where I sit, daydream, watch

long-tailed tits flit in and out of mature willow whips,
listen to blackbird's perfectly honed pitch,
the distant echo of a reply. I take it in, gulp it down
like a hummingbird hawk-moth starved of nectar.

The Art of Listening

Hunt out wild flowers,
reach out, not to pick them
but as an offer of intimacy.

Stay open-hearted,
don't put your ear
to the ground to listen

for sap or soil, instead
tune into the words
written between the lines –

visible in the way bluebell,
pink campion, stitchwort
offer up their secrets,

have made themselves
vulnerable against
pale and dark greens.

This is an offering –
last chance to hear
this moment's prayer.

Come and Go of Relationships

Yesterday Mull's landscape was seductive,
wind's salty smell was tinged with
zest of sea kale, horned wrack.
A small spot of sunlight shone on the sea,
like a shoal of silver fish celebrating,
or rippled mercury.

Today goose down snow is falling
as if Cailleach and her hags
are ripping into each other
with over-stuffed pillows.
Congealing clouds
dull smells, quell sounds;
Mull is veiled,
then shrouded
in white.

Lovesick

I'm a poem without words –
have no stanzas to hold me up,
no aliveness of alliteration,
timing of rhyming.
I crave the curves of vowels,
certainty of consonants,
but only why and what if
go round and round my head –
baggage too heavy to lift off the carousel.
I try to convince myself
I don't need words,
they're just letters
vacuum sealed in boxes.
Other times, when shafts of moonlight
funnel through cloud,
the mynah bird inside my heart strains
with her small repertoire of words,
bows her head.
She knows the tune well
but can't find the words.

Speed Dating with the Divine

He's explaining why the boiler wouldn't work.
I'm paying full attention,
I think.

His voice fades.

The contours of his face soak up light,
are ever more present,
more enchanting.

Warm honeyed milk with a hint of chilli
volcanoes from my gut through my heart
spreading a beauty in its wake
that engulfs everything.

Everything?
Including me?
A self-conscious giggle …
BAM!!
I'm hearing his voice
*… and all because of the thermostat
so that was a surprise, wasn't it.*

It certainly was, I reply truthfully,
most unexpected.

Blade of Grass
(after Brian Patten)

She asks for a poem,
is offered a blade of grass.

She doesn't marvel at
its struggle through earth,
the mystery of its greenness,
instead she points out
anyone can give a blade of grass.

She doesn't press it to her heart,
dry it, keep it in a locket,
instead she claims
the offering is absurd.

Words, like a blade of grass held taut
between edges of thumbs,
can squeal or make music
depending on the force of the breath,
and whether your ears are primed
for pain or pleasure.

Remembering Patrick
(for Patrick Whitefield)

I remember his wide-awake feet,
how they trod without crushing grass,
his earth-stained hands
smiling as they cupped soil,
his greenhouse warmed by chicken heat.

I remember his red neckerchief,
loose jacket with benevolent pockets,
his thistle-down voice
confident as bindweed,
lavish as willow leaf.

I remember his heart caught on thorn,
his body bent like buckler fern,
face furrowed, eyes misted
for vandalised home of vixen, badger,
dwindling habitat of fawn.

I remember towards the end
how people he'd touched,
gathered together, heads bowed
to whisper his name in prayer.

What I can't remember now
is whether his eyes
were grass, earth or sky.

What Remains Unspoken

Yes, it was me who cleared
my throat on that hot June day
as we pulled into the platform,
said the man in the worsted suit.
The sun had layered light with dust
magicked her shape into being,
as it had been the hour of our parting –
dress bright as a buttercup,
hair drawn back from her face,
eyes misted to an unfamiliar blue.
She pressed a letter into my pocket.

I saw her place the letter in his pocket,
said the station clock.
It was the bright sunshine dress
that caught my attention,
so at odds with how they were;
their fingers lingered, parted only
when arms ran out of stretch,
eyes kept contact until
time and space overtook them.

She waited too long for his reply,
said the picket fence.
I heard she married Tom Brackley,
the post mistress's son.

The steam couldn't comment,
it had been lost to the air, unlike
the flavour of their unspoken words
which still clings to the brickwork,
is stored in the memory
of the willow and meadowsweet
around Adlestrop.

When everything's quiet
it doesn't mean
nothing's happening,
said the poet's ghost.

Mixed Portfolio after Death

I am the cartographer;
I map the face of the son who has lost his father –
the sinkholes, avalanches, volcanoes,
the doldrums that intervene
between endless emails.

I am part of the production team;
I help sort out venue, costumes, scenery,
resuscitate forgotten Old Testament hymns,
produce the script for the last curtain call
before the main character exits to Verdi's Requiem.

I am the art curator;
I am dismantling a temporary collection –
Swedish bookcase, hand woven carpets,
pairs of re-soled Church's shoes,
wife's lace-trimmed underwear,
yards of stacked-just-in-case yoghurt pots.

I am the meteorologist;
I forecast a slow moving cold front,
months of grey skies
interspersed with sudden storms
and downpours.

Grief

Under cover of darkness
a baboon climbed in
through a gap in the brickwork,
made himself at home in my house.
He's upturned my vase,
scattered sunflower petals
over the sofa like sterile confetti,
bombed the floor
with my best Royal Doulton
and half-eaten fruit.
Banana skins skulk, like black ice
waiting to bring me down.

In this mess
I have no appetite.
I pace, unable to stay seated.

When I leave the house
his shadow clings to my back.
Just as I start to forget
he rummages through my hair
as though I need to be groomed.
In the silence of the night
he whispers your name
then adds:
is gone forever.

Wake-up Call

A hover fly, a horse fly, a house fly,
a blue bottle, a bumble bee,
any honey-bee-like buzzing
snatches my attention,
knocks all side-thoughts
back into storage.

Walking on the Machair after Snow

The gods have been up to their tricks,
have laid down a green felted cloak in the night,
tacked it to the earth with dandelions, violets, celandine.
Rocks poke through unstitched seams, and
sun has magicked melted snow into sequined stars.
The wind strums the five stringed fence,
has transformed its usual drone into a love song.
I know this is where I belong.

The Wind Lets Us Know Who's Boss

Strong gusts have layered brown spent bracken
like thatch over the ground. Rushes are tired
of the east wind, have formed a queue along the water's edge,
are creeping towards shelter on the opposite shore.

The wind catches the back of my throat, I lean into it, force
myself forwards, head bent towards anywhere that might
have a mobile signal, strain to hear your chopped up
voice over the roar –

fish supper – Simon – *chickens' fence* – *asthma attack* –
some event has been *postponed* – snippets of your life
I can't slot together, like an incomplete jigsaw puzzle
without its picture, tipped out on the floor.

Life's too Short

I watch starlings strutting in high winds.
The glint on their mother-of-pearl backs
rivals the sparkle of sun on sea even though
their feathers are ruffled.

I step outside, oust my grouchiness,
dump my grumpiness, rest my head
against warm granite, join a peppering
of flies just passing time.

And on the Seventh Day

No wind.

The lake is holding its breath.
      A downy emerald arches her abdomen,
            lays eggs on floating debris.

A moorhen pushes its neck forwards,
      pulls it back. The ripples behind it part company
            in perfect symmetry.

A painted lady lands on heated stone,
      gives a slow round of applause with her wings,
            folds them together in prayer.

Damselflies glint like splinters of stained glass
      A broad-bodied chaser idles on willow.
            I barely breathe.

A carp jumps.

Hooked on Iona

A mosaic of smoothed, not quite round pebbles give way
as my feet touch them. It's as though fragments of
grey and pink evening clouds have been laid on the ground
just for me to walk on.

One pebble stands proud, I pick it up, move it from hand
to hand, curl it in my fingers, promise not to keep it too long
from birdsong, place it deep in my pocket.

I search out their ancestors – rocks covered by cropped grass,
clean chiseled granite, boundary stones laced with lichen,
watch how their offspring – shingle, sand, are tossed by sea,
separated by wind.

Where saints preached, pilgrims prayed, I'm courting
this pre-prayer, pre-breath dynasty, tracing a line back
to our shared ancestors, getting to know
the long-lived branch of my family tree,
the one that won't know
extinction.

Nothing about the Birds is Ordinary this Morning

With the whole sky available
a rook trailing straw in its beak
passes so close to my face we

almost collide and the sparrows
that take flight each morning
from the willow opposite

St Oran's Chapel stay put
and several steps further
a swarm of starlings fly low –

crown me with iridescence,
land on a nearby fence
and even though the rhythm

of my footsteps is out of tune
with their tiny heartbeats, they
don't even twitch as I pass by,

behave as if I am one of them,
accept me without checking
whether I have wings,

or sing starlingeze, their gaze
so trusting, so generous,
I feel del-i-cious,

can taste my own sweetness,
like the early days
of a new love.

This Being Human

On Iona I don't sleep.
St. Columba and his disciples –
did they really cross the Irish Sea in a coracle?
Weren't their families worried?
Did they know how many days it would take?
Did their clothing keep out the rain?
How did they bail out water?
Was it difficult to navigate around the rocks?
Did they eat? Or were their vision and prayers
enough to sustain them?
I toss and turn prodded by so many questions.

At home I do sleep –
my head can't take in the idea
of thousands in rubber dinghies
on treacherous seas,
hundreds in the water
with only enough breath
for one final prayer.

Mountain too High to Climb

Behind his colourful mask
the mandrill's eyes are glazed.
Once he was suckled,
carried skin to skin.
Once he crowed over
a cacophony of howler monkeys,
foraged for fruit,
on steaming ground.

In this dry landscape of olive trees
his troupe has been replaced
by a wattle and daub shell.
He's chained at the ankle –
a full stop
w a i t i n g
for his sentence to end.

My inner mother wants
to tear down the cage, unchain him,
reunite him with his family,
but the mother on the outside is worn thin,
held together with frayed thread.

As my three small children,
fed up with mandrill's face,
run towards an eruption of carp,
I'm pulled to chase after them,
find I've turned my back on the mandrill.

Embroidering

She moistens the end of the blue silk thread with saliva
before pinching it between thumb and forefinger.

She holds the needle's eye against white, pushes, then pulls,
makes sure the lengths are even, winds one end

round her moistened finger, rolls her thumb across it,
ties a knot. She's already blanket stitched

the raw edges of the linen, now she's decorating the middle
in satin and cross stitch. When it's done

she'll lay it over the bruised table handed down from
her grandmother. Meanwhile sewing helps pass the time

while she listens out for waking children, waits for
the man of the house to return from the Pig and Whistle.

This Being Human

On the Edge

Together they walk.

For him, the khaki lake holds
shape-shifting shadows of New York skyline,
towers ripple-cut by squabbling helmeted ducks,
fractured limbs of alder provide hide for fleshy predators,
hanging, watching, waiting to strike
while bulrushes march unnoticed into water's territory.

For her, walking in different shoes,
the green lake is full of life,
a breathing space, a delight.

Crossing Boundaries

He's cocksure, in tight jeans, preened quiff.
She's an iridescent fledgling
shimmering in sister's silk, mother's make-up.

        He motions her onto the floor.
            They shake heads, dance chest to chest,
        cavort like crested grebes.

She knows the moves from Strictly.
He's perfected them with intent,
suggests they go somewhere more lively.

Car stops in a deserted spot.
As helpless as a finch caught by sparrowhawk,
she buttons her bill, lowers her lids,

        lets her imagination take flight,
            merges with a murmuration,
        ballooning in the dusking dark,

lands with a string of starlings,
smells beech bark, tastes beech breath,
feels the certainty of beech branch.

Years later when
men
begin felling beech trees

        she protests, lashes out,
            unbuttons her beak,
        screeches *Rape!*

How It Was

Eleanor never left space in
her non-stop monologue
for me to ask about her life,
she sprayed out words like bullets
from an automatic rifle:
I've been spat on, called nigger,
told to get back to the jungle ...

In the same kitchen where
she mopped the floor, I
decorated candied oranges,
studded them with cloves,
criss-crossed them with red silk ribbon,
offered one to Eleanor.

She hooked the ribbon
with her forefinger, held my gift
away from her body
like a grenade about to explode.

I found out she lived in
the overcrowded part of Notting Hill,
when someone flick-knifed
the latch on her sash window.

The papers only said she'd died,
didn't say who'd done it, or why.

This Being Human

Cream Tea with Ginger Baker

Minutes before high tide
I'm sipping a strange brew,
warming my hands on the cup,
watching waves being
chased by a storm.

When the wind, not satisfied with
shuffling brushes, banging mallets
on any taut skin it can find
begins felling dustbins.
A sea surge starts a drum roll...

a wave, higher than you
ever got on cocaine,
SMASHES its crash cymbals
against the seawall.
The beach café rocks!

Takes me back to that white room –
walls throbbing,
floor pounding,
bodies bobbing,
heads banging,
drumsticks working
up to a crescendo …

Wan anything else luv?

My grip loosens
on the lukewarm cup.

Exactly the same again … please.

Injected Wisdom

The bee's venom reaches my jaw,
let's me know there's no need to speak –
the landscape is much more articulate.

Light Plays with the Mute Button

It's as if silversmiths
have been up all night melting metal,

have poured it into the bay.
I follow its flow as it mingles with pewter.

Stunned by the simple play
of light on water, my mind's chattering

has run out of fight, resumes
only when sea turns a uniform grey.

On a Teenage Death

Up to my neck in the hot tub
I take in the distant horizon as
clouds over the mountains lower themselves
onto the breast of the goddess.

Reeds stretch towards the shoreline,
hang their heads, as though
they're embarrassed, would rather
not share in this intimacy.

My playfulness ends as the wristband
holding my locker key tugs, hauls
me back to myself – it's similar to
the watch strap that he wore.

Reminds me that unlike the clouds,
he has no more horizons to meet,
places to settle, will never again
lie heart to heart with a goddess.

Journeying

I walk with eyes
washed by loss,
silence stuffed into
every unstitched pocket.

The distance between
me/grass,
me/sky,
me/granite
has shrunk so much
I feel their nakedness fizz
on the back of my tongue.

It's difficult to believe
that usually my eyes slide over
this same grass, sky, granite.

Holding Heraclitus' River in Mind

I tear a piece of sea kale, place it on my tongue.
It's as fleshy as navelwort, feels awkward
against the roof of my mouth.
I bite down, nudge it from left to right.
Its bitterness is less intense than dandelion,
lacks the lemon-kick of sorrel.

I slide the pulp around my mouth, bring
my teeth together, grind it over and over
like a cow chewing the cud. When the last
tinge of a tang has melted, I swallow, notice
as it slides down my throat. The aftertaste
is bittersweet, like every delicious,
never-to-come-again moment.

Hammering It Home

In this warning wind
    sent by disgruntled gods,
        sorrel, alexanders, campion
           although flattened, stay rooted.

Me? I'm shoved backwards,
    moved on faster than I want.
        Gusts suck, blow up a gale
           in my anorak, as if to rip it to shreds.

It drags my hair out of my hood,
    whips it across my face,
        accuses me of fueling its fury.
           I accept my guilt, bow my head.

On Feeling Overlooked

The beauty of the place won't let me rest, insists I go to
the North Beach despite continuous torrents.

A pair of doves feeling the pull of spring stay on the Abbey lawn,
don't follow the rest of the flock to St. Oran's Chapel.

A scoop of whistling swallows wave their wings so fast
they look like bats who've mistaken day's dullness for dusk.

A wagtail sprints across an invisible line, the only competitor
in a race, stabs the ground, pulls out a morsel, gannets it down.

Waves carry garlands of bladderwrack inland as a gaggle of geese
head south over darkened sand dunes pitted by rain.

And me? I'm taking in these delights and noticing how easy it is to
take for granted the carpets of wild irises that haven't yet flowered.

Some Habits are Impossible to Break

This morning
I'm not going to dress myself in a to do list.
I'm going to stay in my pyjamas, be answerable only
to gulls' squawk, sparrows' chit-chat.
I'll hide poems in unexpected places,
turn somersaults with the wind,
skim water in a cormorant cloak.
make myself small enough to fit inside a snail's shell,
savour the passages I've underlined
from *Love in the Time of Cholera,*

And tomorrow
is going to be completely list free –
I'll just stay in bed
eat chocolate,
drink whisky,
read *One Hundred Years of Solitude*
until the light fades.

Difficult to Grasp

I don't mind
           that barely-held
stones give way,
               my feet slip,
     knees collapse,
               body slides
          belly down
     over tough
rough terrain
          again
          and again
as I struggle to the summit.

I don't even mind
          that parched grasses,
     cut my hands
          as I grab at anything
     to slow my fall

               What I do mind
          is how quickly I lose that fullness,
     that bubbling over of heart filling chest
          once I no longer see
          buzzards' underwings splayed
          against solid blue of sky.

Difficult to Grasp

Sunflower from a Still Life
(after: Vase with Twelve Sunflowers January 1889, Van Gogh)

Severed from my roots, I don't have long to paint a portrait
of this blue-smocked man, palette knife in hand.

In this dark-moon chamber he darts with to and fro dragonfly
frenzy, enough to unseat stars, set them spinning.

Fiery stubble claws around the edge of his bandage, threatens
to overheat, feed his fever, consume him.

Black eyes, like crows over a wheat field in constant flight,
are stark against the landscape of his face.

He daubs yellow, not of sun, but nicotine, bruised skin, bile,
sallow chair nursing only pipe and pouch.

I search for anything to ease my disquiet in this space
bereft of warmth, bee hum, dance of breeze.

What kind of man is this that turns his back towards
the light, whose face doesn't follow the sun?

Reflections on Narcissus

I'd like to pull this son of a river god out of the mud,
hose him down. I think he's been maligned –
think about it, how often does pond water stay as still as glass?

There's pitter-pattering of drizzle, pummeling of storm,
rippling as demoiselles land on waterlily leaf,
tadpoles hide from heron, water boatmen row, row, row.

Maybe it was the different qualities of light, essence of water,
chance to hear fern's breath that held him there.

Maybe he fell in love with every face he saw – wrinkled faces,
flat faces with long chins, squashed noses, stretched mouths.
Maybe he was the first enlightened being.

Maybe Narcissus shouldn't be associated with a disordered
personality. After all, if you look at the flower you'll see
a yellow halo surrounds its tiny face.

Difficult to Grasp

Loss of Voice

Beyond the orchard a small army of volunteers
are harvesting willow.

Creeping buttercup, dandelion, water mint
have become casualties to the mud.

Willow stumps stand in regimented lines. But
it's not this scene that troubles me –

I worry that long-tailed tits, warblers, wrens and
even the mistle thrush near the sky line

will give up on love songs, tunes to mark
territory, unable to compete with

crunch of loppers,
drone of chainsaw,
crack as timber gives way.

At the liberation of Belsen my father told us
he was struck by the absence of birdsong.

There wasn't even an alarm call.
And that's all he said.

Sparrow Thin

Forgive me,
I just can't do this anymore,
I'm stuffed, stuffed so full I'm stiff,
like the taxidermist's bird trapped under glass –
such a grotesque object.
It's what I do, who I am
I regurgitate food into gaping white bowls in public toilets,
like an exhausted gannet feeding its young
worn ragged by constant demands,
round and round
I go.
I go
round and round,
worn ragged by constant demands.
Like an exhausted gannet feeding its young,
I regurgitate food into gaping white bowls in public toilets,
it's what I do, who I am –
such a grotesque object.
Like the taxidermist's bird trapped under glass,
I'm stuffed, stuffed so full I'm stiff.
I just can't do this any more.
Forgive me.

Sparrow Thin.

Difficult to Grasp

The Importance of Telling the Bees when a Death Occurs

Before sunrise place your ear against the hive, tap gently
three times. As the faint buzzing becomes more audible,

send warm breath across the entrance holes to announce
your arrival, lower your voice to a whisper, pass on

news about the death. The bees won't feel numb,
wander around fretting, they'll do their waggle dance,

pass the message through the colony. They'll know this is
not the right time to swarm, or to starve the queen –

she'll need all her energy to hold the colony together.
After Russian soldiers invaded my mother's village,

shot the men, raped the women, no-one told the bees –
worker bees fed too many grubs royal jelly, a procession

of queens led swarm after swarm, each smaller, less viable
than the last   until the main colony collapsed.

Freudian Reaction

As bee toxin oozes out through my pores
I spend hours in the hotel bathroom.
Scent of bee death sticks to my skin
despite frenzied washing, it lingers
like the blood on Lady Macbeth's hands.

I rebuke the face in the mirror, vow in future
not to let my hair fall forward, allow it
to trawl near my hive. I reach for an elastic band
on the sink edge, tie my hair back,
show my commitment to make amends.

Leaving the North Beach

I want to eke out its last gifts before I'm
ferried back to where
I call home.

I undress my feet, soak up the warmth as
I might absorb the heat of a lover's
flat palm.

I take in the salty air, sound of lulling waves,
the slight give of ground under
my weight,

step around driftwood, channelled wrack, kelp,
bones of something
I can't name.

And something, that might or might not be me,
is unearthing untold stories held
between my breaths.

That this dialogue might never happen again
stings the backs of my eyes,
births a yearning.

I pocket a pebble – not serpentine green
but selkie grey, the shape
and size of an eye,

and I *leave* the imprint of my raw heels
splayed toes – a map
of my passing.

I know now that although migrations will
come between us, I will
keep returning.

Going Home

On waking, I look across the sound.
The mainland is fog-bound, unknowable.

Suitcase packed, I stand staring out to sea.
A silver streak of light lands on water,
leaches into slate –
three hundred million white birds
are readying themselves for flight
over and over, without taking off,
as if they're not sure whether to risk
journeying home.

Then, only then, I recognise
the source of my own stirring.

Travelling at Speed while Sitting Side by Side

Taxi arrives. Whether it's because I can't bear
another half-heard conversation or because
a taxi driver saved my skin last night, I take the front seat.
The driver's nervous. I ask where he's from –
Shiraz, Iran, he says. I mention Hafiz. He recites
one of his love poems. We melt into it.
He offers me the names of similar poets.
I jot down – Walad, Razi, Tabrizi.

I ask whether his partner minds him working late.
Details gush out – he's thirty-seven, wants children,
lots of them, has dated many women, can't find
the right one, time is running out, he's fallen out of love
with driving taxis, has been in Glasgow sixteen years,
is going home in June with a one way ticket, hopes
to find a bride in Shiraz, his mother and sister
already scheming.

All this heart-felt longing tipped into my lap
in the six minute journey, falls onto the pavement
as I step out of the cab and we make eye contact –
he becomes the taxi driver, I take on the role of passenger.
I pass him a ten pound note, wait for the change.
We say our polite goodbyes
as if we're strangers.

Grace

Sometimes
it's difficult
to have faith
that the dark moon
will shine full-faced again.

Then in the jumble
of petrol pumps,
concrete, lines of lorries,
a full moon beams,
oozes brightness,
reminds those listening
that tides breathe
even on the blackest night.

On Arriving Home

Only a pinprick of puffiness persists.
My swollen eye has been replaced
by a swelling of deep gratitude
to the small bee who surrendered her life,
interrupted my usual vision.

Indigo Dreams Publishing Ltd
24, Forest Houses
Cookworthy Moor
Halwill
Beaworthy
Devon
EX21 5UU
www.indigodreams.co.uk